W9-CNC-078

MIND BENDERS
Adventures in
Lateral Thinking

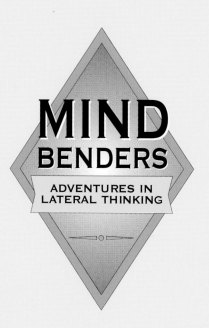

MIND
BENDERS

ADVENTURES IN LATERAL THINKING

Devised by
David J. Bodycombe

With an introduction by
Victor Serebriakoff
Hon. President of International MENSA

BARNES
&NOBLE
BOOKS
NEW YORK

This edition published by Barnes & Noble, Inc.,
by arrangement with Robinson Publishing

Formerly published under the title *Lateral Puzzles*

The use of copyright clipart originated by
Corel Corporation, Techpool Studios Inc., One Mile Up Inc.,
and Image Club Graphics Inc., is acknowledged.

1999 Barnes & Noble Books

ISBN 0 7607 1254 9

Printed and bound in Singapore

03 M 9 8 7 6 5

INTRODUCTION

By Victor Serebriakoff,
Hon. President of International MENSA

The father to the idea of lateral thinking is Edward de Bono, a past Mensa member and an old friend. I have chaired many of his brilliantly informative lectures to Mensa audiences. His lectures are as unusual as they are visual. He uses a projector and a reel or two of transparent film for a continuous succession of rapidly drawn sketches to illustrate his always fascinating talk.

His use of so much illustrative support is implicit to his whole theory of communication and problem solving. Verbal communication and linear logical thinking is very limited. A single string of words or other symbols is all that can be sent or received. But the continuous stream of sketches De Bono makes sends out whole arrays of messages, and the information transfer rate is vastly increased. You learn more, and learn it faster, by such a method.

De Bono's advice to the solver who is utterly baffled is to stop trying to solve the problem by analytical steps, by the normal process of breaking it into comprehensible pieces. Lateral thinking is to allow one's mind to wander off in a number of apparently irrelevant directions, in a mode closer to that of day-dreaming than to hard thinking. By this means, the solver will mobilize the enormous and often apparently irrelevant semantic connections from any thought complex that exists, often below the level of consciousness in the human brain.

Let me give an example from my own experience. I had a line of machines making wood mouldings. These mouldings were dropped into bins which were emptied and transported further down the production line. When we had spent lot of money building the system, I was in great trouble because I had overlooked an important problem: as the pieces dropped, they were damaged by the impact of their fall into the bin. There seemed to be no solution and we considered giving up the whole scheme at a great cost.

I found the solution by going in the opposite direction to the obvious one. I stopped asking how to avoid the impacts, and instead asked the opposite question: "How can I make each piece have *more* impacts as it falls?"

It utterly puzzled the workmen with whom I discussed this. "That will only make matters worse," they said. Then I explained: "If the piece collides several times, it will disperse the energy of its fall over several, much less damaging impacts." We simply arranged a few sloping boards to intercept the fall of the piece so that it was deflected from each to the next – the problem was solved.

Lateral thinking puzzles are those where the mind reverts from the normal verbal and symbolic mode and goes into the right side of the brain, where thinking is holistic and can take much more into account. This is thinking in a multiple parallel mode, where many factors are taken into account by giving each of the factors some kind of "weighting". It is much akin to making a judgement about the suitability of applicants for a job. The best engineers and designers have the lateral thought approach.

The many problems and conundrums set here are designed to test your ability to turn away from a problem and let your mind wander around in almost every direction, except the one that seems most obvious. You will find some very challenging teasers here, but if you can ask yourself the right kind of question you will find you can solve them.

I think I can promise you several ecstatic "Eureka!" moments if you accept the challenges here in this lateral thinking adventure.

The illustration shows a system of five cogwheels.

The number of teeth on each wheel is shown. How fast should you try to turn wheel X if you want wheel Y to revolve at a speed of 15 revolutions per minute?

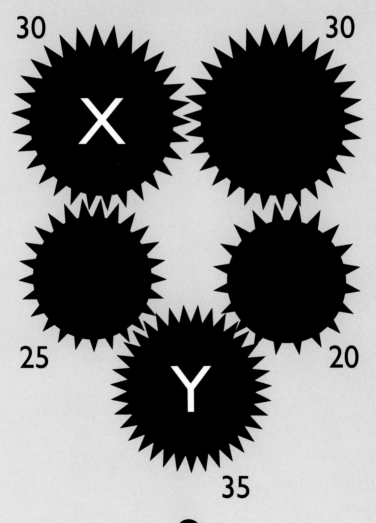

30

30

X

25

20

Y

35

This sequence of letters and numbers is much more familiar to you than you might think. Have a good look down the list then see if you can provide the missing first term.

???????
2 TD
3 FH
4 CB
5 GR
6 GAL
7 SAS
8 MAM
9 LD
10 LAL
11 PP
12 DD

Last year, several of my friends went on holiday. Three friends caught some winter sun. Bridget chose Barbados, Louis said he enjoyed Mauritius, and Victoria went to the Seychelles.

Kath was my only friend to venture into Asia, having gone to Nepal for a month. Raj wanted to explore the new Bosnia-Hertzegovina, Sofia trekked across Bulgaria, and Cyprus was the destination of choice for Nic.

Ron went to Botswana, Rob to Kenya, and George to Guyana. George also went to the Cayman Islands later in the year.

Of course, by now you'll be able to tell me where Don went, won't you?

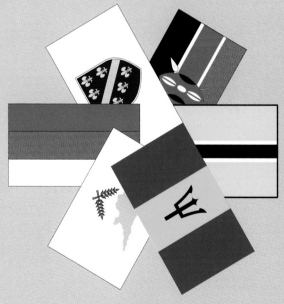

It's not an easy life being a zoo keeper. I can't begin to imagine how they tell all those penguins apart.

To see if you should apply to your local zoo for a job, I'll supply an initial aptitude test. Here is a pair of pictures of a panda, and there are two clearly visible differences between them.

Identify both of them.

Anagrams have long been a popular topic for puzzle writers, so it seemed fitting that I should include one in this book also.

What is the **longest** word that you can make out of the following letters, using each letter once at most?

PACHINKO

The sentence shown in the circle of letters below seems like nonsense. In fact, each word shares a special property with all the other words.

Can you discover the hidden logic?

Two people were discussing the matchstick puzzle shown below. The idea was to move only one match to make the statement correct.

"I reckon it's impossible to make it exactly correct," claimed Kevin, "unless you cheat by turning the equals sign into a 'not equal to' sign."

"Maybe," said Mandy, "but I can make it approximately correct." She made her move and the result was only a few percent from being exactly correct.

"Aha!" exclaimed Kevin. "I can move the same match as you've just moved to make the statement even closer to being exactly correct."

Can you work out what the two solutions were?

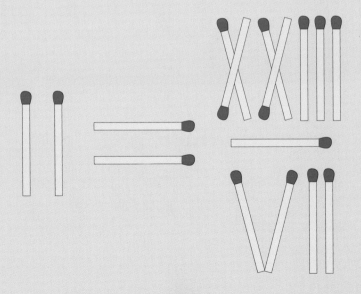

Look carefully at the picture below, because there's a hidden sequence somewhere in there ready to leap out at you.

Work out the logic used to create this diagram.

The earliest form of crosswords were word squares. In this puzzle, your challenge is to complete this 4 x 4 word square so that valid English words can be read across and down each row and column.

To make things easier, we have filled in one letter and provided the remaining fifteen letters on sets of tiles, which should be positioned into the grid. How could you possibly fail?

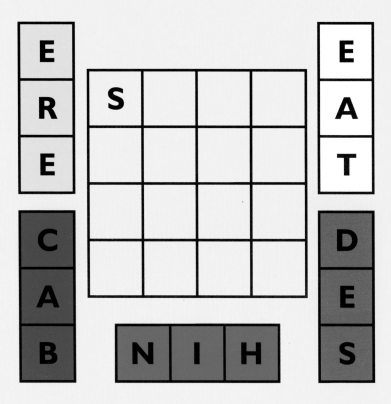

Continuing the crossword theme, here's a standard crossword that I've nearly finished. However, the remaining clue is proving to be rather puzzling. The unsolved clue is printed below the grid.

Can you discover the diabolical trick used by this final clue?

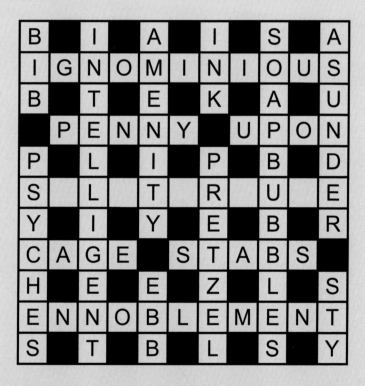

B		I		A		I		S		A
I	G	N	O	M	I	N	I	O	U	S
B		T		E		K		A		U
	P	E	N	N	Y		U	P	O	N
P		L		I		P		B		D
S		L		T		R		U		E
Y		I		T		E		B		R
C	A	G	E		S	T	A	B	S	
H		E		E		Z		L		S
E	N	N	O	B	L	E	M	E	N	T
S		T		B		L		S		Y

Sadomasochism (anag., 4)

A few years ago in Britain, it was illegal to sell certain items on Sundays. Goods which were timely or perishable in some way (such as newspapers and fresh fruit) could be sold. However, goods which did not become less useful over short periods time (such as books and home improvement equipment) could not.

How did hardware stores get around the law?

This must surely be the world's easiest game of I-Spy. I'm spying, with my little eye, something beginning with 'H' from the illustration below. To make things a little harder, I'm only going to allow you one guess.

So, make your choice then look up the word I'm thinking of in the answers section.

Place these sixteen pawns into the squares on this chessboard so that there are a maximum of two pawns on any row, column or ANY diagonal – that is, not just the longest, main diagonals. One pawn per square maximum.

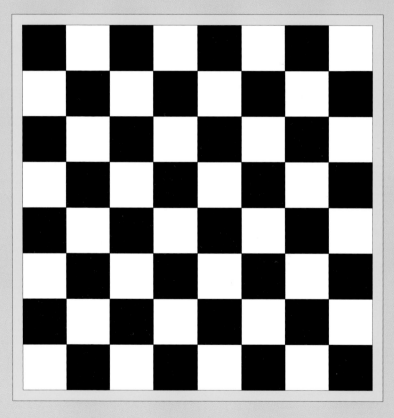

What is the reasoning behind this mathematical expression in picture form?

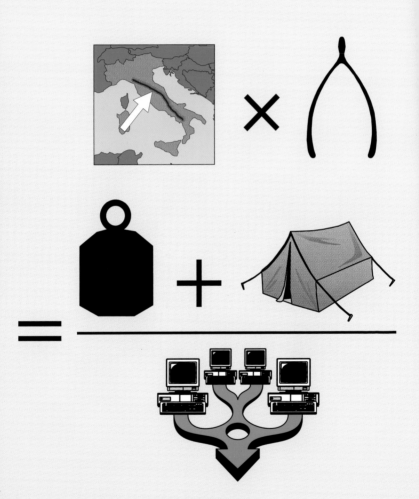

You've probably seen something similar to this before on standard IQ tests. You have to work out what goes between the parentheses in order to complete the first word, and begin the second word.

What is the answer?

As I'm feeling in a particularly generous mood at the moment, I'm going to tell you the answer to this puzzle. It's "seven".

Now you've got to work out the question. To help you, you can use this maze, and move one square in any direction each time. I've also highlighted the start and finish positions for you.

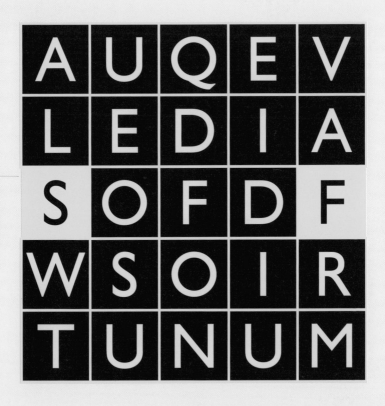

Simply match up the pictures to the words. There's a particular sort of person that would find this puzzle very easy.

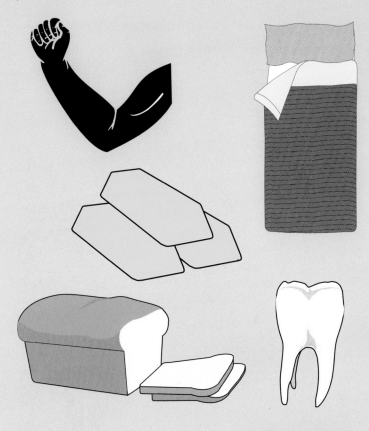

LIT   DENT
OR
BRAS   PAIN

These three yellow circles have a blue segment painted on them. The circles are rotating at three, four and five revolutions per minute, as illustrated below.

How long will it be before the circles are positioned so that the large triangle is complete?

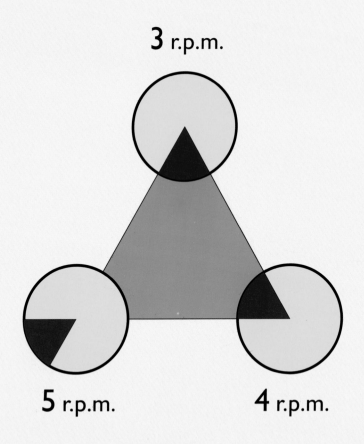

3 r.p.m.

5 r.p.m.   4 r.p.m.

This is a word game that's trickier than it looks. I would like you to make the longest word you can using only the six letters illustrated below.

Your answer must be a well-known English word, and you are not allowed to use any letter twice.

Think you've got a good answer? I can virtually guarantee that my solution will slay your effort.

Draw one continuous solid line around this maze in order to connect the letter A to the letter B.

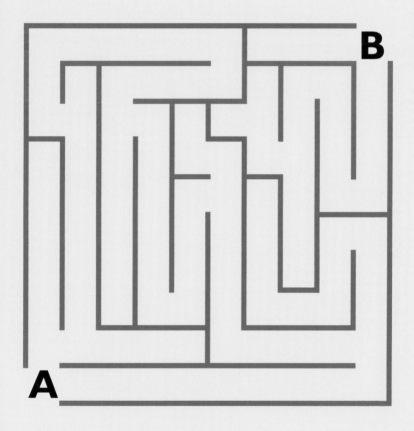

Apart from being 15-letters long, these two words have something in common. Furthermore, they are the longest two words that have this property.

What property am I talking about?

PARASITOLOGICAL
OVERIMAGINATIVE

Here are a number of different words which, as anyone can clearly see, are all to do with food and culinary implements.

What is the more lateral connection between these words?

FOIL

FORK

PIKE

MARTINI

SPONGE

PINEAPPLE

FROG

KNIFE

ONION

WHIP

GRAPE

SQUID

BARREL

In the game of snooker, players attempt to pot any one of the fifteen red balls, followed by any of the six higher scoring balls, followed by another red and so on until all the reds have gone. After that, the yellow, green, brown, blue, pink and black are potted in sequence. A miss means the other player gets a turn. The points value of each ball is shown below. It is not hard to calculate that the maximum possible score in one turn is 147 ($[1 + 7] \times 15 + 2+3+4+5+6+7$).

"That must be a terribly difficult score to get in just one turn," said Eddie to his playing partner.

"Not so," argued Seamus, "for I can think of a different score which is the hardest to get by far, because there are less possibilities available to the player."

What number is Seamus thinking of?

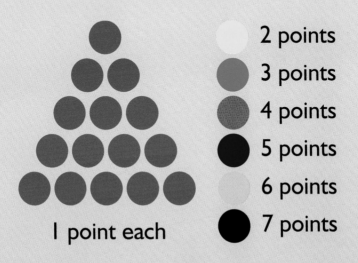

1 point each

2 points

3 points

4 points

5 points

6 points

7 points

This simple mathematical teaser requires more lateral thought than you might think.

Given the cost of all the combinations shown, how much would the fourth ring cost?

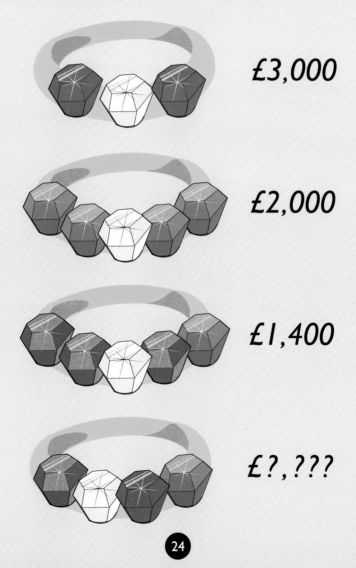

£3,000

£2,000

£1,400

£?,???

I have a calculator that displays digits using LCD seven-segment displays like so:

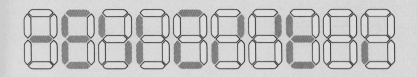

and that can also display arithmetic symbols like so:

$$\times \quad \div \quad = \quad - \quad +$$

It is currently displaying:

$$3 = 5 + 1$$

and I can tell that one of the segments in the display of one of the digits is not working.

Which one?

If you thought the previous puzzles have been quite fruity, you haven't seen anything yet.

Take a good look at the grid, then tell us what fruit should go in the empty box.

PEAR	PINEAPPLE	MANDARIN
?	AVOCADO	NUT
BANANA	APPLE	STRAWBERRY

Have a careful look at this sequence of diagrams, and then see if you can identify which diagram from the five options provided should replace the question mark?

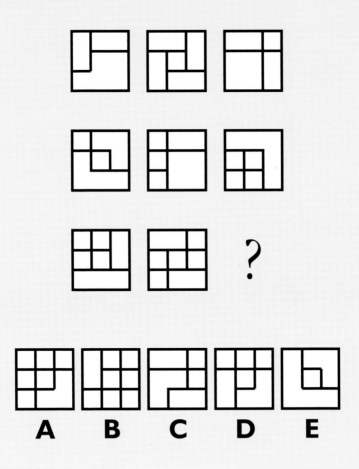

A   B   C   D   E

How many parts of this four-part challenge can you solve? In each case, a valid equality must be formed by adding a given number of straight lines.

PART 1: Add one line to this sum to make it correct.

$$8 - 2 = 13 - 3$$

PART 2: Add two lines to this sum to make it correct.

$$8 / 2 = 13 - 3$$

PART 3: Add three lines to this sum to make it correct.

$$\frac{8}{2} = 13 - 3$$

PART 4: Find the alternative solution to Part 3.

There is one mention of five, ten and fifty in the word search shown below. Can you find them?

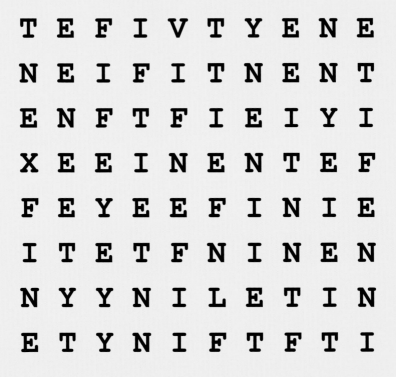

```
T E F I V T Y E N E
N E I F I T N E N T
E N F T F I E I Y I
X E E I N E N T E F
F E Y E E F I N I E
I T E T F N I N E N
N Y Y N I L E T I N
E T Y N I F T F T I
```

If it takes three rabbits to eat three carrots in six minutes, how long would it take a rabbit and a half to eat a carrot and a half?

A particular type of puzzle that is very popular at the moment are "alphametic" puzzles, where a series of numbers and letters represents a well-known phrase or saying. Here are some examples:

52 C in a D
(52 Cards in a Deck)

7 D a W
(7 Days a Week)

13 in a BD
(13 in a Baker's Dozen)

So, what do you think this stands for?

5 W in the A

Some philosophers are arguing as to whether everlasting love or a single £1 coin is better.

How did the monetarist philosophers win the argument?

Pointillism is an effect whereby lots of small dots of different paints or inks are placed very closely together. At a distance, these dots would have the effect of looking like a solid shade.

The technique was mainly developed by Georges Seurat, and his most famous pointillism painting is *Sunday Afternoon on the Island of La Grande Jatte* (1886).

When is the last time you have seen pointillism in action?

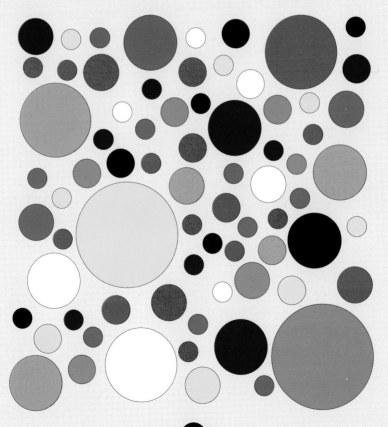

The bucket on the left contains some sand, the other bucket contains an identical amount of rice.

With my eyes closed, I bet I can tell you which bucket holds the sand without touching either bucket, or any of its contents, in any way, shape or form.

How is the trick done?

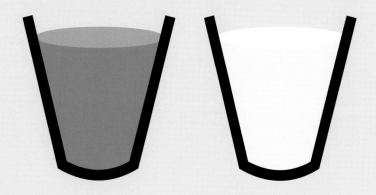

I heard on the radio that researchers had found that two-thirds of all cars carry only one-third of all people being transported by car.

Assume that all the vehicles in the survey were standard family cars that can accommodate a driver and up to three passengers.

Even from that limited information, you will be able to *deduce* whether the research was precisely correct or whether the researchers were approximating their result.

A secretary at a firm that made leather fashion accessories (such as belts, handbags, etc.) accidentally came into a lot of money. A huge number of social security deposits were made by a large number of different people under her account number. All the deposits would have been millions of dollars, enough for her to retire on. However, the mistake was soon spotted, although the same problem continued to recur for several years afterwards.

The secretary did nothing fraudulent, as she was the victim of many other people's mistakes. Can you think laterally to determine the circumstances in which this could have happened?

Each brick in this pyramid contains a number, and we've already revealed six of these numbers.

The number on each brick follows the rule that it is equal to the sum of the numbers on the two bricks below it. For example, the numbers on the bricks in the second row (in green) will add up to 177.

Using the given numbers, and some inventive thinking, it is possible to calculate the number on each brick. What are the numbers in the bricks along the bottom row?

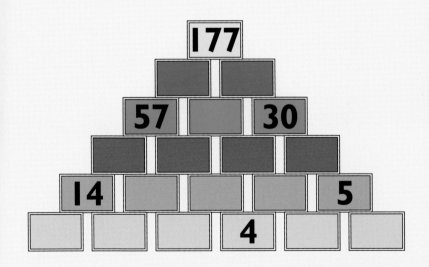

Simply complete this crossword. Or is it so simple?

1	2	3	4	5
6				
7				
8				
9				

Across

1 A completely flat surface.

6 A level of thought or existence or development.

7 Popular method of aerial transport (abbrev.)

8 Tool for smoothing.

9 Type of tall spreading tree with broad leaves.

Down

1 A state of quiet free from war.

2 Otherwise, when all fails...

3 While, when, because, though – used in comparisons.

4 Female fowl.

5 If at it, relax.

John the milkman had a round thirty-pint barrel of milk from which he had already served eight pints to one of his customers. Berry and Benny lived next door to each other and both bought milk from the milkman every week.

Benny had a four-pint jug and Berry had a five-pint pail that they used to store the milk in. However, this week, Berry only wanted four pints of milk and Benny only wanted three pints.

John hadn't brought his own measuring instruments with him. How did the three of them arrange it so that they each ended up with the amount of milk they wanted, and no milk was spilt during the transactions?

4pt.

3pt.

What is the logic behind this sequence?

Libya

Canada

France

India

Central African Republic

South Africa

To prove, if proof were ever needed, that authors are humans too, here's an instance when I was caught out by my own puzzle.

In a previous book, I posed the question shown below and readers were invited to think of the simplest possible answer to the question.

The intended answer was FOUR, because there are four letters in the word "FOUR". This is the only number for which this property holds.

However, a friend of mine pointed out that there was another perfectly good, straightforward answer to the same question. Can you work out what the alternative is?

How many letters are there in the correct answer to this question?

What are the elusive characters? Missing two letters or numbers?

W A T E ?

M ? L O N

London has always been a very popular destination for tourists from all countries.

However, in which of the following famous London locations are you always sure to find a Scandinavian?

Tower Bridge
Hyde Park
St. Paul's Cathedral
Greenwich Meridian
Camden Market
Houses of Parliament

What is the lateral connection behind the creation of 10-pin bowling, mime artistry and ice-cream sundaes?

Bonnie and Clyde are the only two players left in a poker game using an ordinary pack of fifty-two cards. They each get dealt eight cards and make the best poker hand they can using any five of them they like.

Bonnie boasted that she had a straight – in other words, five cards whose numbers were in sequence, missing none out. Clyde was certain that Bonnie was bluffing.

What cards must Clyde have held in order to know that Bonnie wasn't telling the truth?

For the purposes of this puzzle, assume that people are equally likely to be born under any sign of the Zodiac.

There are twelve signs of the Zodiac. How big a group of people would you have to be in before it was more likely than not that at least two of the people present shared the same birth sign?

What is the lateral connection between these items?

I buy a particular brand of tire for my car that will last 20,000 miles before it becomes unsafe to use. I expect to travel 50,000 miles by car this year, on long-distance business trips.

Given that I start the current year with new tires on the car, and that I will be able to get by safely with only eight tires this year, how can this be done?

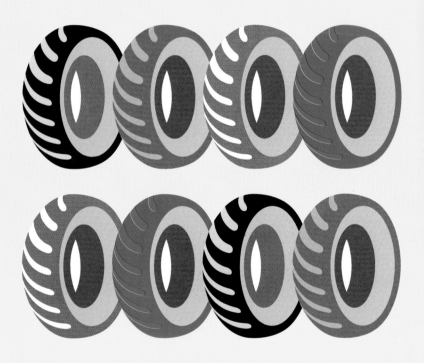

Has there ever been a case of a gold medallist in the Olympic games having more legs than average, but fewer arms than average?

As I was walking into town today, I saw one weapon, two tissues, three oak trees, four sea shores and five housewives.

How many oranges would I have seen?

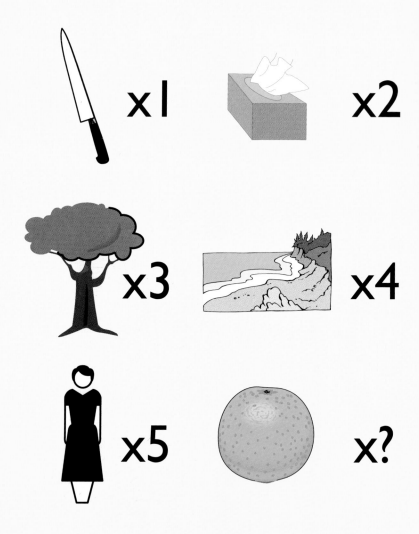

Not including the words in the question, or the page number, there are **six** words on this page. What are they?

RED

BOLD

ƎƧЯƎVƎЯ

NARROW

ITALIC

Samantha was having an enjoyable week touring the country taking photographs of open-air mazes for her next book. She arrived at one country house which had a maze made out of patio tiles.

"If you can get from the START to the FINISH, by passing over only white tiles and avoiding all the black tiles, then I'll let you photograph my house," said the property owner.

How did Samantha complete the challenge without even moving any of the tiles?

Using exactly three 2s, three 3s and three 4s, fill in nine squares in this grid so that every row and column come to the same total.

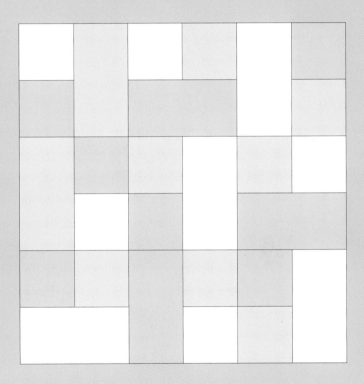

Here are nine matches, which have been arranged on a table to form a figure which looks like a cube.

Suppose two of the matches were removed. How could you rearrange the matches that remained so that they still formed the figure of a cube?

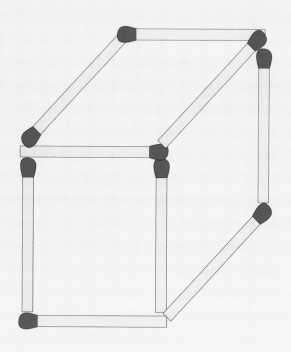

And we stay on the theme of matchsticks for our next puzzle.

This time, you have to remove three matches so that the result of what remains comes to "3".

How do you do it?

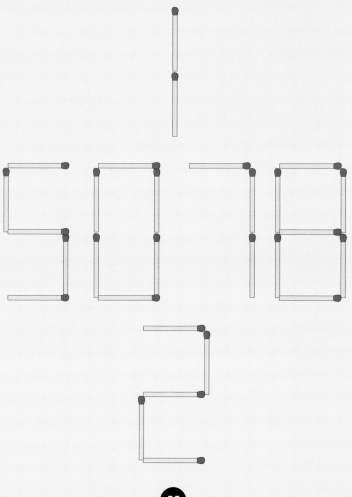

Which **one** of these four symbols is the odd one out?

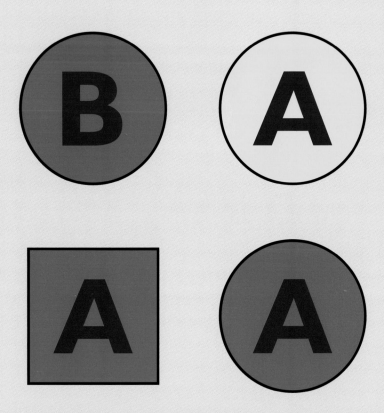

What four letters should replace the blank in order to complete this analogy?

H is to GRAM as D is to ____

I have a very special watch, where each hour is marked off using letters instead of numbers.

Using the watch, can you work out the answers to the clues shown?

12:05 Insect

2:55 Marine animal

8:10 Frosty

3:50 Rot

2:15 Dirty

8:55 Part of a church

Opposites are normally just that – words that have completely different meanings.

However, some opposites are not as mutually exclusive as they may seem. For example, take the opposites "tall" and "short".

I can think of at least two things that can be tall and short *at the same time*. See if your guesses match with mine.

What is the lateral connection between these pictures?

Here are seven little words. You have to pair six of them up to form three little words. The seventh word is a red herring.

Which word is not used?

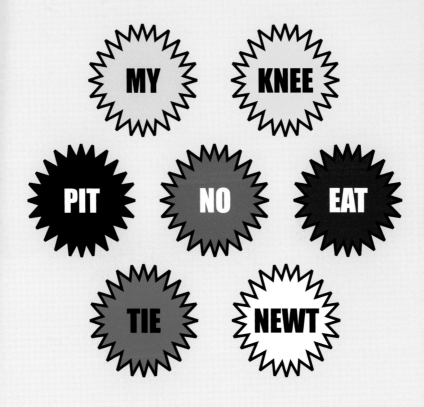

I want to paint the fence around my garden in nice bright yellow. However, after rooting around in my shed, I find that I only have tins of red, green and blue paint.

What would I need to do?

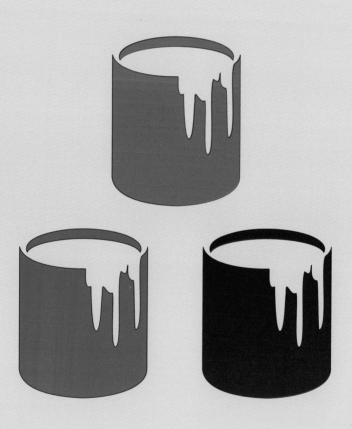

Allen Smithee must be one of the most prolific film directors in the world. Since 1969, this name has appeared on more films than any director you can name. However, it seems strange that you probably haven't seen him being interviewed, or nominated for any awards.

Can you think why this might be?

Here is a series of letters. The letters are in a particular order, and there is a hidden logic. However, I can guarantee that any standard approach to solving this will almost certainly fail.

So, can you find how this sequence was arrived at?

"S K A L N T"

Once, long ago, the king and queen of an African land were fleeing from power, after an uprising. However, they managed to find a friendly tribe, who lived in grass huts.

The king and queen asked the tribe if they could store their seats of power, for fear that they would be destroyed should any of their political opponents find them. The tribe agreed to do this while the king and queen went into hiding for a few days.

However, some anti-monarchy tribesmen found out about this and burned down the huts containing the seats, destroying everything the tribe had.

What corruption of a well-known proverb sums up this story?

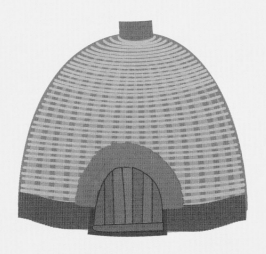

There are ten numbered statements printed below. How many statements on this page must be true?

1. *The number of false statements is one.*

2. *The number of false statements is two.*

3. *The number of false statements is three.*

4. *The number of false statements is four.*

5. *The number of false statements is five.*

6. *The number of false statements is six.*

7. *The number of false statements is seven.*

8. *The number of false statements is eight.*

9. *The number of false statements is nine.*

10. *The number of false statements is ten.*

Make up a three-digit number by selecting, in any order, three digits from the grid so that no two of the chosen numbers come from the same row or column.

Now test to see if that number is divisible by 3. What is the probability that your number is **not** divisible by 3?

Claire runs the quiz at her local tavern for the benefit of the regulars there. However, in this week's quiz there was quite an amount of controversy.

Why was Claire in so much trouble?

THE GOOSE AND GANDER PUB QUIZ

Q1) Who invented the steam engine?

Ans.: James Watt

Q2) In what year was Einstein awarded the Nobel Prize for his theory of relativity?

Ans.: 1921

Q3) Who popularized the terms "evolution" and "survival of the fittest"?

Ans.: Charles Darwin

Q4) What was Cinderella's slipper made from?

Ans.: Glass

Q5) What was Glenn Miller's signature tune?

Ans.: In the Mood

Q6) What is the capital of Nigeria?

Ans.: Lagos

Q7) Which English king signed the Magna Carta at Runnymede?

Ans.: King John

Draw two straight lines across the diamond so that the total of the numbers in each of the resulting four regions is the same.

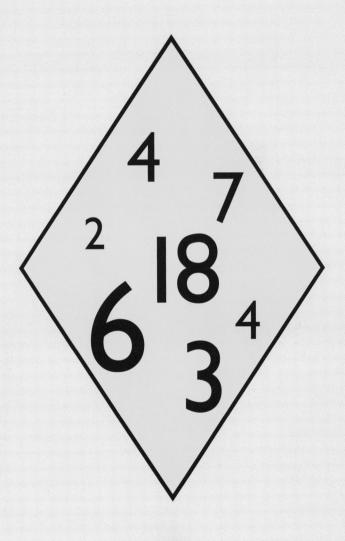

Here's an interesting crossword to complete. As you should know by now, in this book things are not as they first seem...

Across

1 Pure delight (3)
4 Croupier (3)
6 Cunning (3)
8 Four score (2)
10 Beverage (2)
11 Oil company (2)
12 Ferrous metal (2)

Down

2 Wearisome (3)
3 Marine animal (2)
5 From the Middle East (4)
7 Latin for "I see" (3)
9 Part of a cake (2)

An in-joke in the office in which I work is that we tend to use rather a lot of TLAs.

Can you guess what a TLA is?

In this diagram, I have illustrated six particular objects. Study the logic carefully, then give an example of an object that could take its place in the middle segment.

Solve the crossword.

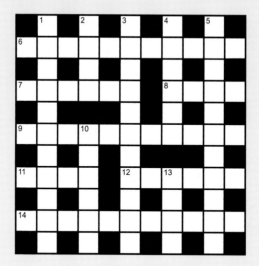

Across

6 Leisure pursuits. (11)

7 A calculated risk designed to gain an advantage over an opponent. (6)

8 The sharpest point of a corner. (4)

9 In a puzzled way. (11)

11 Metallic element used in the galvanization process. (4)

12 Be plentiful. (6)

14 Contradictory to the expected outcome. (11)

Down

1 Counting system which uses groups of sixteen. (11)

2 To paint coarsely. (4)

3 A war machine, mainly used as a metaphor in modern times. (11)

4 The ending. (6)

5 Between lines. (11)

10 Hand-held weapon (U.S. spelling) (4-2)

13 Date of death. (4)

To solve this puzzle, find the treasure.

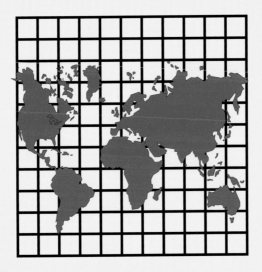

To locate the treasure, discount five locations.

Do not look in the sea or on the border.

If the solution does not seem obvious, shed some light on it.

Whatever remains, X marks the spot.

Here are some famous quotes attributed to literary, film and television characters. In each case, can you identify in which book, film or programme these quotations are to be found?

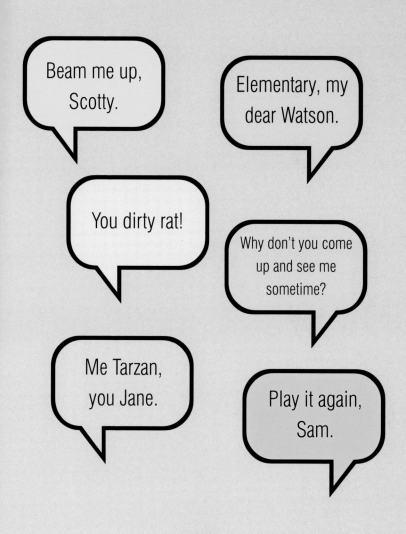

Beam me up, Scotty.

Elementary, my dear Watson.

You dirty rat!

Why don't you come up and see me sometime?

Me Tarzan, you Jane.

Play it again, Sam.

Where is there a definite mistake on this page?

When it is pointed out to you, I think you will agree that it is a definite mistake.

2 is the smallest prime number

70% of 70% is 49%

–4 minus –7 is equal to 3

8 divided by ½ is equal to 16

0 is an even number

How many of these diagrams can you trace without using any line twice or taking your writing implement off the paper?

A woman is touring a magnificent Tudor mansion which has only one door where visitors can enter or exit.

The first room she starts in has an odd number of doors to adjacent rooms. She follows the tour guide around all the exhibits, and doesn't pay much attention to where she has been or where she is going.

When she reaches the final room, which is different from the first room she started in, she notices that this room also has an odd number of doors in it. The guide announces that this is the end of the tour, because they have now seen the entire house. During the trip, they had gone through every door in the house exactly once.

What can you deduce about the number of doors in the rooms in the rest of the house?

Sandra sets the quiz for the local social club every Thursday. However, on one particular Thursday night she had forgotten to bring her quiz questions with her, and she couldn't remember a single question from it.

Ever the improviser, she asked each of the ten teams to write down five questions for her to ask. Then she would use these fifty questions in the quiz.

However, there was naturally a danger that every team would set impossible questions, which wouldn't make for a fun evening out. So how could she rig the scoring system so that every team had a fair chance of knowing the answer?

Here is one of those sliding block puzzles. The idea of the numbered variety of this puzzle is to get the numbers from 1 to 15 to read in order across each row.

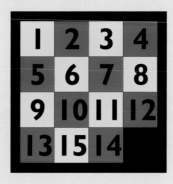

A famous American puzzler called Sam Loyd once offered a large amount of money to anyone who could solve the sliding block puzzle if the 15 and 14 were interchanged, as shown. He could do so without damaging his wallet, because it is impossible to achieve.

However, is the block puzzle below impossible to solve? Your aim is the same, but with non-consecutive numbers: arrange the tiles so that they read in increasing values across each row.

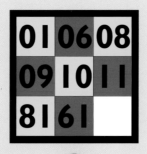

Sword Words are anagrams of each other. For each of the clues below, find a pair of Sword Words.

Example: **Dinar currency** would give you **TUNIS UNITS.**

The coding of the spaces should confirm your answers.

3 letters

Rodent culture?

4 letters

The final wooden support

5 letters

Prime cut of fish

6 letters

Speedier desserts?

7 letters

Keep the coffee flask warm

8 letters

Anonymous door-to-door merchants

A master hires servants to keep his grain accounts. The master would pay the servants $70 for every day that the servants kept his accounts properly, but would fine the servants $100 for every day that they didn't.

After 16 days, the master says the servants owe him $30.

On how many days did the master keep his grain accounts properly?

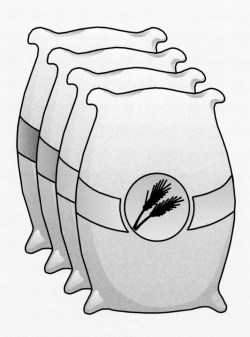

Which of the odd ones out is the odd one out?

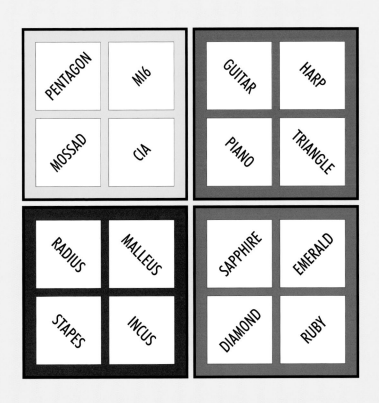

PENTAGON	MI6
MOSSAD	CIA

GUITAR	HARP
PIANO	TRIANGLE

RADIUS	MALLEUS
STAPES	INCUS

SAPPHIRE	EMERALD
DIAMOND	RUBY

What flag should I use to illustrate the final word to continue the logic?

ORATION
TAXES
NOVA
STERNUM
AMANITAS

How many changes need to be made to this arithmetic statement in order to make it correct?

First answer the six general knowledge questions. Then work out the lateral link between the answers.

What type of small hound was primarily bred to chase hares?

Which group of Ecuadorian islands in the Pacific takes it name from six species of giant turtle?

In mathematics, what name is given to the point of the graph where the axes meet at zero?

In biological classification, what is the smallest category, several of which make up one genus?

Which is the generic term for a scientific, speculative explanation for a principle under investigation?

What means "a monkey with no tail" and "to imitate"?

I claim that the word shown below is a palindrome.

For those of you who are seasoned puzzlers, you would know that a palindrome is a word that reads the same backwards and forwards (such as **madam**, **noon** and **rotavator**). However, it appears at first sight that **footstool** is not quite a palindrome.

In what way can I claim that I am right?

Some of the letters on this keyboard have been eliminated already. To eliminate some more, answer the general knowledge questions about music. You can eliminate the first letter of your answers from the keyboard.

When you have finished, only eight keys should remain. What eight-letter word can be typed using each key once?

1) Dance with three beats in the bar (5)
2) String instrument, name means "Quiet, loud" in Italian (10)
3) Old keyboard instrument, usually associated with women (9)
4) Austrian stringed folk instrument plucked by fingers and a plectrum (6)
5) Bamboo pole, approximately 4 feet long; the player does "circular breathing" (10)
6) In musical scores, it is equivalent to half of a crotchet (6)
7) Like 2, but the strings are plucked instead of struck (11)
8) The glockenspiel is a member of this instrument family (9)
9) Alpine singing style (9)

PASSWORD: ☐☐☐☐☐☐☐☐

Cut this circle into two pieces using a straight cut. Then repeat so that you now have four pieces.

If you have chosen correctly, you will be able to find four related words, one on each "slice".

Here are some *antigrams*. See if you can work out what an antigram is from these examples.

EVIL'S AGENTS

REAL FUN

NICE LOVE

NO MORE STARS

Which black word on this page could replace the question marks in order to continue the logic?

RE

RED

RODE

?????

ADORER

EARDROP

PREDATOR

PORTRAYED

STORE **DETOUR**

RATIO **ROOD**

ROTOR

DARES **AIDER**

Fill in the blanks in each case. The same logic should apply to each sentence, and the sentences are in approximate order of difficulty.

My friend brings me an _____ _____;
"But I want a hot dog!" _____ _____.

Mother's _____ _____ was brightened up when her son said he scored a _____ _____ in the test.

As a bank, _____ _____ money to people so that they can say "One day, _____ _____ this house outright."

_____ _____ costly running shoes when you can opt for ordinary _____ _____ instead?

The man took all _____ _____ _____ to the vet. The fee was $26, which he paid with _____-_____ _____.

I've got one of those new cook books which contain recipes specially created for microwaves. Today I'm making "Soya and Beansprout Surprise".

The instructions are the correct ones for the power of my particular oven (750 watts). The recipe says that I should put all the ingredients into a microwavable casserole dish and heat on full power for 60 seconds.

However, I set the microwave for 64 seconds instead. Why might I do this? (It's nothing to do with the merits of ensuring your beansprouts are nice and hot.)

The manufacturers of the EZ-Fuse™ guarantee that their standard fuses take one hour to burn. However, due to their inconsistent composition, if you cut them in half they do not guarantee how much each piece would burn for. For example, the first half might burn for 40 minutes, and the second half for 20, but you do not know that.

How can you time 30 minutes using only a knife, some matches and the fuse? You may light or cut the fuse as many times as you like – assume this can be done in next to no time.

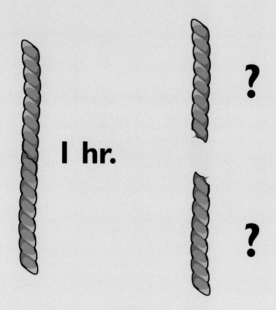

I hr.

?

?

Here, all the letters of the English alphabet have been put into groups according to a particular logic.

What is that logic?

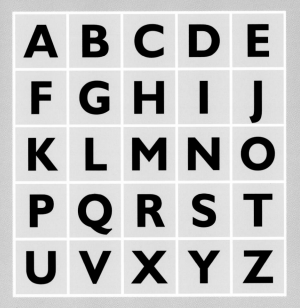

W

Here are some proverbs – sayings that have been passed down the ages as examples of great wisdom, right?

Look carefully at this selection of famous proverbs and you'll see what nonsense that is.

Too many cooks spoil the broth.

Beware of Greeks bearing gifts.

Curiosity killed the cat.

Faint heart never won fair lady.

Great minds run in the same channel.

One man's meat is another man's poison.

Save for a rainy day.

Many hands make light work.

Never look a gift horse in the mouth.

Tomorrow will take care of itself.

Fools think alike.

Sauce for the goose is sauce for the gander.

The meek shall inherit the Earth.

Seek and ye shall find.

Y
Z
E
P
T
G
M
k
1
m
n
p
f
a
z
y

Here I've written the number **1** in the middle of a column of letters. You will notice that there is a gap in the series, which is a particular missing letter. I want to know what the missing letter is.

Hint: if you don't know the answer, I could offer you fifty-two tries and you would still not get it.

I claim that these are the most useless words in the English language. I don't think they tell you very much, and there are other words that would be more accurate.

Think carefully about the meanings of all these words and you will agree with me. Maybe.

CUSTOM

CLIP

MISS

SANCTION

BILL

QUANTUM

SKIN

STRIKE

FAST

TRIM

There's nothing wrong with this fictional story in itself. It uses a lot of acronyms (abbreviations using the first letters of words), but again that isn't the connection we're looking for.

What is the specific common link between all the acronyms used in this story?

I wanted to find out the ISBN number of a particular book I wanted, so I logged onto the Internet. My IBM PC computer is a little old – it uses programs written in BASIC code, running under the DOS operating system.

I was running short of cash, so I went to the nearest ATM machine. I entered my PIN number and the LCD display asked me how much money I wanted. I took out £50.

I found the book I wanted, which was about the SALT treaty. This concerns the decommissioning of ABM missiles that are placed all over the world.

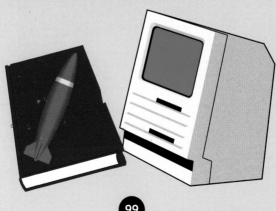

So great is the anticipated demand for this book that I'm already writing 500 puzzles for my next great literary tome.

I'm quite pleased with myself so far, because I have completed 400 of them already. On the downside, I have only been writing, on average, four puzzles a day when I should have been writing thirty-five puzzles a week in order to meet my deadline.

How quickly do I have to write the rest of the book in order to appease my editor?

ANSWERS

ANSWERS TO PUZZLES ENDING IN –1

1 You can try as hard as you like – cog Y won't budge an inch because you need teeth of equal spacing on each wheel for the system to work. Even if this criterion was met, the adjacent cogs will pull it in opposite directions:

11 The hardware store sold apples for £49 each. For each purchase, they gave away a free step ladder! However, this is no longer necessary as Sunday trading in Britain is now legal.

21 Each of those words alternates vowel–consonant or consonant–vowel. These are the longest words that contain this property.

31 Five words in the answer.

41 0.

51 The first five words are RED, BOLD, REVERSE, NARROW and ITALIC. The sixth word is INVISIBLE!

61 PIT + EAT = "Petite"; TIE + KNEE = "Tiny"; MY + NEWT = "Minute". Note that these three words all mean "little". NO is the red herring.

71 Most of our products and services have three-word descriptions, so we refer to them using abbreviations which use the first letter of each word. Appropriately, TLA stands for "Three-Letter Acronym".

81 The answers are: RAT ART, LAST SLAT, SKATE STEAK, FASTER AFTERS, SMOTHER THERMOS, NAMELESS SALESMEN.

91 Each time, a letter is added and a new anagram is formed. The only black word on the page that can fit the sequence is ORDER, which appears in the question ("...marks in order to...").

ANSWERS TO PUZZLES ENDING IN –2

2 AAPIAPT (And A Partridge In A Pear Tree). Each line makes up a line from the song The Twelve Days of Christmas.

12 The word I'm thinking of is "horizon". Did I win?

22 They are all words that describe terms for weaponry. For example, a "pineapple" is the slang term for a grenade, a "foil" is a sword, "grape" are small round bullets and a "pike" is a medieval spear.

32 The first group argued "Nothing is better than everlasting love", but the second group retorted "And £1 is better than nothing." Thus, logically £1 is better than everlasting love.

42 There are two letters missing, and they are C and T. The sequence is the first letter of every word in the question (What Are The...)

52 She took a photograph of the maze, and then solved the maze using the photographic negative. On the negative, the black squares appear white and vice versa. Hence, Samantha could go from Start to Finish using the white squares only!

62 I'd need to go to the hardware store and buy some yellow paint. It is impossible to make yellow from any combination of red, green and blue paint. This is why red, blue and yellow are the three primaries for pigments. Red, blue and green are the primaries for light.

72 Anything that could be associated with WHITE, such as wine or sauce. The other pictures represent a Pink elephant, Red-eye, Yellow Fever, Green fly, Cyan-ide and Blue cheese.

82 None! Not only did the servants keep the master's accounts for him, it's impossible for the servants to keep accounts correctly and wrongly on a combination of sixteen days and end up owing the master thirty dollars, so he had kept the account of how much he owed the servants wrongly as well.

92 Each time, the same sounds fill both sets of blanks but with different spellings. The first one is: "My friend brings me an ICE CREAM; 'But I want a hot dog,' I SCREAM." Similarly: (2) "Mother's GREY DAY was brightened up when her son said he scored a GRADE A in the test"; (3) "As a bank, WE LOAN money to people so that they can say 'One day WE'LL OWN this house outright.'"; (4) "WHY CHOOSE costly running shoes when you can opt for ordinary WHITE SHOES instead?"; (5) "The man took all TWENTY SICK SWANS to the vet. The fee was $26, which he paid with TWENTY-SIX ONES."

ANSWERS TO PUZZLES ENDING IN –3

3 Each of my friends went to a capital city which contained their name:

BRIDGETown, St. LOUIS, VICTORIA, KATHmandu, saRAJevo, SOFIA, NICosia, gaboRONe, naiROBi, and GEORGEtown twice.

So, Don went to England (lonDON).

13 The answer is probably a lot simpler than you might think (there are other arrangements that are also acceptable):

23 The number 2. In a 147-break, the player has a large number of possible combinations, but the only time it is possible to score 2 is by potting the yellow after all the reds have been cleared from the table.

33 When looking at this book. The printing technique used in the manufacture of this book relies on the principle of pointillism.

43 You'd be sure to see a Scandinavian in Camden Market, because "CamDEN MARKet" contains the whole of Denmark!

53

63 There is no such director as Allen Smithee. This name was introduced in 1969 by the American Society of Cinematographers to be used as an anonymous pseudonym whenever the director did not want his name to be associated with the film.

73 **Across:** 6 Relaxations,
7 Gambit, 8 Apex,
9 Perplexedly, 11 Zinc,
12 Abound, 14 Paradoxical.
Down: 1 Hexadecimal,
2 Daub, 3 Battlewagon,
4 Finale, 5 Interlinear,
10 Pick-ax, 13 Obit.

83 **Yellow**: The Pentagon is a
covert government agency.
MI6, Mossad and the CIA
are all secret services.

Red: A triangle doesn't have
strings.

Blue: The radius is in the
arm, the other bones are in
the ear.

Green: Diamond is an
element (carbon), the
others are compound
crystals.

Of these odd ones out,
radius (in the mathematical
sense) is a line whereas the
others (diamond, pentagon,
triangle) are 2-D figures.

93 I know that the microwave
turntable takes 16 seconds
to make one revolution, so
when the 64 seconds are up
the handles will still be
pointing in the right
direction for me to take out
my dinner without touching
the hot dish.

ANSWERS TO PUZZLES ENDING IN –4

4 The two differences are:
(a) The lower panda has a pink toe on his left foot
(b) They are printed on different parts of the page.

14 The pictures all contain numbers: wishbONE, neTWOrk, apenNINEs, TENt and wEIGHT. Hence: $9 \times 1 = (10 + 8) \div 2$.

24 Finding the value of each type of gem is impossible. However, it is still possible to find the price of the ring.

The three rings can be expressed like this:

$0G + 0B + 2R + 1W = £3,000$
$0G + 4B + 0R + 1W = £2,000$
$3G + 1B + 0R + 1W = £1,400$

If we multiply the first line by 1½ and divide the second line by 2, then total all three rings we get:

$0G + 0B + 3R + 1½W = £4,500$
$0G + 2B + 0R + ½W = £1,000$
$3G + 1B + 0R + 1W = £1,400$
_____
$3G + 3B + 3R + 3W = £6,900$

From this, we can see that a ring comprising of one stone of each type would cost £6,900 / 3 = £2,300.

34 Blow on one of the buckets. The differences in the noise between rice and sand hitting the floor will easily identify the contents of the buckets.

44 They were all created as work-arounds to legal bans. 10-pin bowling was created when 9-pin bowling was banned; mime artistry was created in France when the emperor prohibited plays; and when ice-cream sodas were prevented from being sold on Sunday, the vendors served them without the soda – the "Sunday soda", now known as the ice-cream sundae, was born.

54 Rearrange the matches to form a figure 8, which is the cube of 2.

64 Say the letters aloud and you will find that the first letter starts at the back of your mouth, and the last letter is pronounced at the very tip of the tongue.

74 If the previous puzzle seemed a bit tame, it was because it is used in this puzzle. Hold the page up to the sunlight or a bright lightbulb. The crossword on the previous page should be visible. Of the six Xs in the previous crossword, only one is not in the sea or on the outside border of the grid (the X in Perplexedly). Therefore, you should look for the treasure in Northern Iran.

84 ORATION is an anagram of Ontario, one of the Canadian states. TAXES is an anagram of Texas, one of the American states. NOVA is an anagram of Avon, referring to Stratford-on-Avon, one of England's counties. STERNUM is an anagram of Munster, one of Ireland's provinces. Therefore, AMANITAS should be covered in the Australian flag, because it is an anagram of Tasmania. (Incidentally, Amanitas is a word – they're mushrooms.)

94 If the whole fuse lasts 60 minutes, then burning the fuse twice as quickly would make it last 30 minutes. To burn the fuse twice as quickly, we simply need to light both pieces of fuse at once. When one fuse completely burns out, quickly cut the remaining one in half and light the end of the unlit piece. Eventually, the fuse will become too small to cut and you will have successfully timed approximately 30 minutes.

ANSWERS TO PUZZLES ENDING IN –5

5 The longest word is, in fact, pachinko. It is a very popular game in Japan, a mixture between bagatelle and pinball. (Who said this was the puzzle that was about anagrams?)

15 Put a couple of curved lines between the parentheses to make them into a letter O, thus forming the words WHO and OWL.

25 Look at it upside-down, and it should read:

$$1 + 5 = 6$$

but the bottom-right segment of the 6 is not working, so it reads:

$$1 + 5 = E.$$

35 Suppose there are C cars and P passengers. In the more crowded cars, $\frac{2}{3}$P people travel in $\frac{1}{3}$C cars (an average of 2P/C people per car). In the less crowded cars, $\frac{1}{3}$P people travel in $\frac{2}{3}$C cars (an average of $\frac{1}{2}$P/C per car). This means that the average number of people in the more crowded cars is four times higher than the average of the less crowded cars. Given that a car can only have between one and four passengers, this implies no car had two or three passengers! As this is extremely unlikely, the research is hardly likely to have been exactly correct.

45 All four fives and all four tens. Every five-card straight in an ordinary game of poker must include either a five or a ten, regardless of whether the ace is counted as being low, high or both.

55 Remove the top and top-left matches from the 8, and the bottom match from the 0. Then look at the matches upside down. The message reads 2 PLUS 1.

65 People in grass houses shouldn't stow thrones.

75 The only place you'll find all these quotations is in the *Oxford Dictionary of Quotations*, where they are all listed as misquotations. Capt. Kirk has said "Beam us up, Mr. Scott" but not the version in the question. Similarly: Sherlock Holmes has only said "Elementary" in the books; Tarzan never said "Me Tarzan..." in either the book or the original 1932 film; Humphrey Bogart only says "Play it!"; Mae West said "Why don't you come up sometime, and see me?"; and James Cagney never called anyone a dirty rat in any of his films.

85 It's possible to read the calculation as a correct computation without changing anything. Just hold the book up to a mirror so that it reads:

95 All letters in the left-hand group have one syllable when pronounced.

ANSWERS TO PUZZLES ENDING IN –6

6 Take any word in the sentence. Draw a line from each letter through the mid-point (the O of "OR") and you get a different word. Here, VEX decodes to IRK:

16 The start and finish are indeed highlighted, but the "F" is the start, and the "S" is the finish. The message reads FIVE ADD FOUR MINUS TWO EQUALS..., the answer to which is of course "seven".

26 The missing fruit is a pomegranate. Each row, column and main diagonal contains 21 letters.

36 Based on a true story. When the firm sold handbags and wallets, it did so by including fake credit cards, travel passes and similar cards in order to demonstrate the possible uses of their products. However, the manager used his secretary's real number on the specimen for the social security card. Despite the word SPECIMEN being printed on it in large letters, thousands of people believed that was their real social security number.

46 The answer is "five". Suppose there are two people. The chance that they have **different** signs is $12/12 \times 11/12 = 92\%$. The chance that three people have **different** signs is $12/12 \times 11/12 \times 10/12 = 76\%$, and so on. When you get to five people in your group, the probability falls under 50% for the first time (in fact, 38%). If there

is a **38%** chance that the five people have a different sign, then the chance that at least two of the five share the same sign must be 62%.

56 The symbol at the top-right is an odd one out, because it is yellow and the rest are red. The symbol at the top-left is an odd one out, because it has a B whereas all the others have an A. The symbol at the bottom-left is an odd one out, because it is a square and all the others are circles. Hence, the symbol at the bottom-right is the odd one out, because it hasn't been one of the odd one outs!

66 Two statements are correct. Number 9 is correct, because statements 1 to 8 and 10 must be incorrect. However, the statement in the question that says "there are ten numbered statements printed below" is also right.

76 Try as you might, you won't find anything wrong with the mathematical statements. But you did notice that the page number was incorrect, didn't you?

86 The answers are Beagle, Galapagos Islands, Origin, Species, Theory and Ape. The lateral link between these answers is Charles Darwin. He sailed to the Galapagos Islands on H.M.S. *Beagle*. There, he made observations which formed the basis of his book, the *Origin of Species*.

96 Match up the proverbs by their shading and you'll notice how contradictory they are. For example, you are urged "Seek and ye shall find", yet in another pearl of wisdom we are told "Curiosity killed the cat", and so on.

ANSWERS TO PUZZLES ENDING IN –7

7   The first solution is:

$$3 = 22/7$$

But this is much closer to being exactly correct:

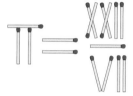

17 Match LIT to the bed, OR to the gold, DENT to the tooth, BRAS to the arm and PAIN to the bread. The English words listed are also French words (Lit is French for "bed" etc.), so a French-speaking person would find this puzzle very easy.

27 The first diagram contains one square (of any size), the second diagram contains two squares (of any size), and so on. Therefore, for the ninth diagram we need option A, which has nine squares of any size.

37 Let us first label the missing numbers:

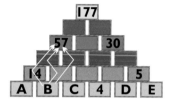

Clearly:
A + B = 14 and D + E = 5

In fact, we can also say:
57 = A + 3B + 3C + 4

This is because there are three different routes up the pyramid where B contributes to the 57 box (as illustrated above), and the same goes for C. Similarly:
30 = C + 3x4 + 3D + E

More careful counting using the some method is needed for the 177 box. There are 5 ways for B (or D) to get to the top of the pyramid, and there are 10 routes for C (or the "4") to reach the summit. Therefore:
177 = A + 5B + 10C
        + 10x4 + 5D + E

We now have five equations to find the five unknown values, which is sufficient. The solution to this system of equations is A=5, B=9, C=7, D=3 and E=2.

47 A saw, a gear, a mouth, a comb and a zipper all have teeth.

57 RTED, so that the words *Histogram* and *Distorted* are completed.

67 0%. No matter which numbers you choose according to the rules, the sum of the digits you select will always add up to a multiple of 3. If the sum of the digits is a multiple of 3, it follows that the number itself will be a multiple of 3 also.

77 The maximum must surely be one – once you've traced your first image you must take your pen off the paper to trace the second!

87 Footstool is indeed a palindrome, but only when tapped out using Morse code!

97 The missing letter is μ, the Greek letter mu. This is why I could allow you to guess from **A** to **Z** and from **a** to **z** ("52 tries") without fear of you getting it right.

The series of letters in the question are the prefixes often used to represent powers of 10. (These are often given in the back sections of dictionaries.) Some examples: the k represents 1000, as in kilobyte; the M represents 1,000,000, as in megabyte. In the other direction, n represents "nano-" or one thousand millionth.

8 It is the prime numbers
overlapping:

$$2357111\,3$$
$$1719232\,9$$
$$3137414\,3$$

18 An eternity – the way the
discs are set, they will never
make a triangle.

28 (1) $8 + 2 = 13 - 3$;
(2) $8 \times 2 = 13 + 3$;
(3) $18/2 = 13 - 3 - 1$;
(4) $8/\frac{1}{2} = 13 + 3$.

38 The solution to all the
Across clues is PLANE.

Down: 1 PEACE (Ps), 2
ELSE (Ls), 3 AS (As), 4
HENS (Ns), 5 EASE (Es).

48 Given the information in the
question, I must drive a car
that only has three wheels.
Changing my tires every five
thousand miles, I use sets of
tires in this sequence: 123,
124, 134, 234, 123, 456,
567, 568, 578, 678.

58 For each time, read the
hour hand letter followed
by the minute hand letter
aloud. Hence, 12:05 is "a
bee"; 2:55 is "seal"; 8:10 is
"icy"; 3:50 is "decay"; 2:15
is "seedy"; and 8:55 is
"aisle".

68 All her questions are based
on misconceptions. (1) Watt
improved Newcomen's
existing engine, but did not
invent the steam engine
itself; (2) Einstein won his
Nobel Prize for his study of
the photo-electric effect;
(3) Herbert Spencer
popularized these terms;
(4) In the original story, her
slipper was made out of fur
– a mistranslation from
French to English caused
the slipper to turn to glass;
(5) It is *Moonlight Serenade*;
(6) The capital is now
Abuja; (7) John sealed the
Magna Carta, but he did not

sign it because he could not write.

78 All the other rooms she visited must have an even number of doors. If you always exit a room via a different door than the one you entered it by, there must be an even number of doors. It doesn't matter if we start and end our journey in different places because we are told that those rooms have an odd number of doors – hence, when we pass through the first door, there are an even number of doors left to use. (Incidentally, if we ended the journey in the same place as where we began, then the starting room must also have an even number of doors.)

88 The answers are: 1) Waltz, 2) Pianoforte, 3) Virginal, 4) Zither, 5) Didgeridoo, 6) Quaver, 7) Harpsichord, 8) Xylophone and 9) Yodelling. Crossing out W, P, V, Z, D,

Q, H, X and Y accordingly leaves you with the password of TRIANGLE, another musical instrument.

98 I claim (lightheartedly, of course) that these words are useless because they can mean two opposite things at once. For example, **strike** means "to hit a ball", but in baseball it means "to miss a ball". To **sanction** something means to agree it, but imposing sanctions mean you're not agreeing. A **bill** is either having money ("dollar bill") or demanding money ("here is our bill"). The term **quantum** leap is popularly used to refer to a significantly large advance in technology, whereas in physics a quantum is the smallest change possible. Something that is **fast** is either quick moving, or not moving at all ("stuck fast"), and so on for the others.

ANSWERS TO PUZZLES
ENDING IN –9

9 Once you work out that the
NIH piece needs to be
turned upside-down, the
rest is easy:

S	H	I	N
C	E	D	E
A	R	E	A
B	E	S	T

19 My word is "assassinate",
which I think you'll find
does not use any letter
twice. Three or four times,
yes, but not twice.

29 The Roman numerals V, X
and L (5, 10 and 50
respectively) appear once in
the puzzle. The words
FIVE, TEN and FIFTY do
not appear anywhere in it.

39 John poured four pints into
Benny's jug, and Benny
poured it into Berry's pail,
giving Berry the four pints

he wanted. There were
eighteen pints left in the
barrel; John poured milk
into Benny's jug until the
level reached from the brim
to the opposite corner of
the barrel, leaving it half-full
with only fifteen pints left.

49 The average number of legs
is just less than 2, because
there are a few people with
one or no legs. So anyone
with two legs has more legs
than average. In a number
of sports over the history of
the Olympics, several
competitors with only one
arm have won gold medals.

59 A story could be short (in
length), but extremely
unlikely (as in "that's a tall
story"). A person could be
tall (height-wise) but short
(as in "short of money").
You might also argue that a
drink could be tall and short
(alcoholic), and a tall cake
could be short (brittle).

69 Split the 18 into two 1s and two 0s:

79 Teams received 1 point for answering each question correctly. Also, for every question they set, they received a bonus calculated using the formula: 10 minus the difference between the numbers of correct and incorrect answers. Hence, if a team set a question where 5 teams were correct, and 5 were wrong, that team received a bonus of $10 - (5-5) = 10 - 0 = 10$ points. If they set a question that was too hard, where only 2 teams answered correctly but 8 answered incorrectly, they would only receive

$10 - (8 - 2) = 10 - 6 = 4$ points. There are similar ways that would achieve much the same result. Based upon a real quiz run by the Oxford University Invariant Society.

89 Cut the circle as shown, to give the words SLICE, EACH, RELATED and FOUR. These are all related words because they all appear in the question.

99 To use the term "ISBN number" is strictly wrong, because the N of ISBN already stands for Number, so "ISBN number" reads as "International Standard Book Number number". Similarly for all the other acronyms in the story.

ANSWERS TO PUZZLES ENDING IN –0

10 The (anag., 4) means that the answer is an anagram of four letters. However, the grid shows that it must be eleven letters long. That's because the answer is "self-torture", which is an anagram of "four letters".

20 One possible route is marked here in blue:

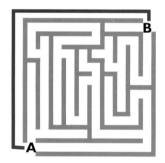

30 Nine minutes. It takes one rabbit six minutes to eat one carrot, and nine minutes to eat one and a half. I very much doubt if the remaining half a rabbit would be feeling well enough to eat anything...

40 Libya's flag is plain green; Canada's flag is red and white; France's flag is red, white and blue, and so on.

50 This isn't a question about rhymes, as it might first appear, but about the number of letters in the word. To obtain the number, you count the letters in the word and take away five. Therefore, the number of ORANGES you would have seen is two (7 letters minus 5).

60 The diagrams represent four anagrams: SPRITES, STRIPES, PERSIST and PRIESTS.

70

Across: 1 XTC (ecstacy),
4 DLR (dealer), **6** DVS
(devious), **8** AT (eighty),
10 BR (beer), **11** SO (*Esso*),
12 IN (iron).
Down: 2 TDS (tedious),
3 CL (seal), **5** RABN
(Arabian), **7** VDO (video),
9 TR (tier).

80 It is impossible to solve the
puzzle as illustrated.
However, it does become
possible if you turn the
puzzle upside-down:

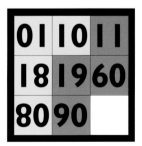

90 Antigrams are anagrams
which relate to the opposite
of their unscrambled
version. For example,
EVIL'S AGENTS gives
EVANGELISTS. Likewise,
REAL FUN unscrambled
gives FUNERAL, NICE
LOVE is VIOLENCE and
NO MORE STARS is
ASTRONOMERS.

100 It has taken 100 days to
write the 400 puzzles so far.
However, I should have
written the entire book in
(500 x 7) ÷ 35 = 100 days,
so I've got to work at the
speed of light to get the
book in on time.